WEIGHT ON ME!

PARRISH MIMINGER

MAJESTIC
MULTIMEDIA COMPANY

WEIGHT ON ME! by Parrish Miminger

Published by Majestic Multimedia Company
P.O. Box 570878
Orlando, FL 32857
info@majestic4us.com

Unless otherwise noted, all Scripture quotations are from the King James Bible KJV - used as public domain

ISBN-13: 978-0996533232
ISBN-10: 0996533230

Printed in the United States of America

$\mathscr{E}$NDORSEMENTS

"Weight On Me" is a must read for any Christian library. Parrish Miminger has within these pages encapsulated (in this easy read) the profundity of the various "weights" in the scriptures for our lives. This book will change our outlook on weight and challenge us to embrace the corrected measures for success!

Dr. Pamela Herndon-Suggs
Senior Pastor, Greater Life Fellowship Church
Raleigh, North Carolina

During my 20-year army career, physical fitness was essential to mission accomplishment. During my latter years, the chaplaincy introduced a program called spiritual fitness.

This book speaks to the disciplines and principles necessary to develop a healthy spiritual body that will enable you to accomplish any assignment given by God and remain dutiful in the midst of all challenges till the task has been completed per policy and protocol (God's Word). In the presence of an unhealthy universal church, this book is a much-needed tool for recovery and revival.

The Reverend Alonzo Braggs
People's AME Zion Church
Palmdale, California

Parrish Miminger is a gifted young man on the literary horizon within Christendom. The Lord has uniquely anointed him with a spiritual perspective concerning weight. Parrish utilizes the concept of physical weight training and body adaption in comparison with how the Lord prepares us for spiritual training.

This book will cause you to take a reflective moment with your own life and contemplate just how spiritually apt you actually are. I encourage you to delve deep into this book and parallel it to yourself. I can honestly say that I am Godly proud of Parrish Miminger and excited about what is to come for him.

Bishop Anthony L. Jinwright
The Gathering at Pneuma Life Center
Charlotte, North Carolina

The words that emanate from the pages of, "Weight On Me", were obviously inspired from our Holy Book. It serves as a great opener and is very inspirational. Parrish Miminger has meticulously disclosed a prophetic freshness and biblical insight that will serve as a spiritual lens for generations to come.

The reader will be taken on a journey that will be life-changing upon applying the spiritual principles. Thank you for writing such an inspiring book that has challenged me to evaluate and reevaluate my spiritual approach to the level of "Weight" that God has bestowed upon me. God knew what I needed. He sent your book. This book is rich and a very timely work written for such a time as now.

Pastor Felicia A. Horne-Murchison
Refuge of Deliverance Ministries, Inc.
Elizabethtown, North Carolina

The new trend in the Body of Christ seems to be spiritual schizophrenia. When we don't know who we are in the Kingdom of God, we don't know where it is that we belong in the Kingdom of God.

We go back and forth in titles, ministries and so forth only because we don't understand our own spiritual capacity and identity. Minister Miminger helps the reader see his or her potential in Christ. *"Weight On Me"* carries an unprecedented weight indeed!

Pastor Edwrin Sutton
Author, TV Co-Host
Smith Metropolitan AME Zion Church
Poughkeepsie, New York

$\mathcal{D}$EDICATION

I would like to dedicate this book to my wonderful mother, Barbara Miminger McLaurin. Thank you for rearing me in the admonition of God. I would not be the man I am today without a Godly mother.

You have always been my greatest supporter. From birth date to present day, you've always encouraged the freedom of expression, while demanding a high degree of excellence. Whether it be in sports, academics, music or ministry, you pushed me to strive for GREATNESS!! I am overjoyed to be your son.

This book is a testament to your excellence as a parent. Thank you for fulfilling your God given charge to, "Train up a child in the way he should go [teaching him to seek God's wisdom and will for his abilities and talents], Even when he is old he will not depart from it."

I Love You Momma!!!

- Parrish

CONTENTS

Foreword by Dr. Nathaniel Wells ……............. xi

Introduction …………………………….... 1

1 Weight Training………………………….... 5

2 How Much Do I Weigh?………………….......... 11

3 The Weight of Oil ……………………….......... 19

4 Carrying Extra Weight ………………….......... 27

5 Following The Liter ……………………… 33

6 Weight of Opposition ………………….......... 39

7 Strength Training…………………….................... 45

8 We Weigh More Together …………………... 53

9 Weight of Opportunity……...…………….... 61

10 The Weight Relationship Carries ………….......... 67

11 I AM the Way …………………….......... 77

Appendix…………………………….......... 85

Author Resources …………………….....…... 87

$\mathcal{F}$OREWORD

Life in Christ is all about growth. If our desire is to succeed with effectiveness on our spiritual journey; we will have to embrace the challenge of the adequate training necessary. Howbeit, one of the most intricate realities in the world today, is the weakness of our ability to seek out strength.

The scriptures institute emphasis on getting a suitable understanding as it relates to wisdom (Proverbs 4:7). When we began to embrace the strength of the Lord, we will soon discover that He has powerful methods of manufacturing our resistance in areas that we may have grown weak in. It is predominantly important to God that we are ever increasing in the rank of our Spiritual growth and maturity (Luke 17:5).

Our greatest participation in the plan of God is by simply acknowledging Him as the "source of our strength" (Psalm 28:7). By doing so, God increases our ability to retain more of Him, which we refer to as "spiritual capacity". To be on the receiving end of such a phenomenon, requires one to practice and embrace the "total reliance" of the ultimate weight trainer and rank increaser – "God".

It is there, through His eternal wisdom, He discloses Himself to the identity of our spirit man; that "His weight or yoke is easy, while His burdens are light" (Matt 11:30). God is strategic...

Naturally, visiting the gym and exercising properly, causes our body to increase in muscle mass, while simultaneously facilitating the shed of excess unhealthy weight. The spiritual epiphany of exercise correlates to the "building of ourselves on our most Holy Faith" – (Jude 1:20); while relinquishing problematic weight that we may be carrying.

For too long, have we strained our spiritual muscles, due to "problem lifting", instead of "power lifting". God desires to upsurge our strength and resistance, giving "power to the faint, and strength to them that have no might" (Isaiah 40:29). When we clasp the many lessons of the "Wait Room", the "Weight Room", will not be as strenuous.

In this timely literary work, Parrish Miminger has captured the practical instructions of understanding the concept of God's training plan. He has unveiled and illustrated the reality of rank in God's world. I highly commend his contribution to the Kingdom of God; and am honored to be apart of his journey.

The best is yet to come,

Dr. Nathaniel Wells
Apostolic Overseer, Construction Zone Ministries International Network
Senior Pastor, Rebirth Christian Center International, Inc.
Orlando, FL

*I*NTRODUCTION

Thank you for joining me on this life-conditioning quest. I seek to empower you, with the necessary tools to accomplish one of three outcomes. Either you will desire to lose weight, tone up or build spiritual muscle. Jesus taught "*No man, having put his hand to the plow, and looking back, is FIT for the kingdom of God.*"

The plow is symbolic of working. Jesus suggests that we should embrace a spiritual workout that causes advancement. By doing so, the exercise will inevitably cause the body to be fit. The Apostle Paul resounded a similar concept of practice when he writes to the

1

Philippian church and says, *"**Work out your salvation**."*

Many times these workouts are a series of trainings that stem directly from a theory known as muscle confusion. This theory suggests that constant change of a workout routine causes the muscles in the body to become "confused."

In term, this increases muscle stimulation by limiting adaptation. The body will never stop yielding results because it never adapts to any one-workout routine.

Spiritually, muscle confusion works the same way. It causes the believer to exercise their muscles by using various techniques and weights. In other words, God will allow the believer to experience extreme resistance surrounding their faith to strengthen it.

"God may test your prayer life; this comes not to break you down but rather to grow you in the area of prayer."

When God wants to strengthen finance, pressure will emerge surrounding your finances. Under diversified training, God intensifies the rate of development within the Body; which yields a well-rounded Body that has the capability of accomplishing anything!!

2

- *Ask yourself, what is my goal for weight training?*
- *Identifying this purpose will give you the scale, of measured effectiveness.*

Primarily, your goal is more associated with your purpose. More specifically, the more effective the training, the more purpose is unveiled. God desires to shape the "Body" of Christ because the totality of who you are is under all of that *WEIGHT!!!*

Your spiritual capacity has limitless boundaries. It grows at a rate, hinged primarily upon spiritual consistency. From prayer to biblical study, the consistent usage of God given tools will exercise and expand your capacity.

As capacity expands, the level of spiritual growth merits an equal level of spiritual release. A legitimate release is only birthed out of conception. In essence, when God releases something through you, it carries the most weight when it is conceived in your womb.

CHAPTER NOTES:

1

*W*EIGHT LIFTING

Weight is defined as: *any heavy load, mass, or object. It can also speak of a mental or moral burden, as of care, sorrow, or responsibility.*

In Hebrews 12:1, the Bible says, "*lay aside every weight, and the sin which does so easily beset us.*" The Greek word for weight, listed here is *ogkos*. It means prominent, protuberance; bulk, mass, hence a burden, weight, and encumbrance. To gain the most from effective workouts, it is best experienced with the assistance of a personal trainer.

In Proverbs 22:6, the scripture gives an indication of the job description for one type of personal trainer. The trainer is spiritually responsible for training *"...up a child in the way he should go..."*. The Hebrew word for child not only makes reference to youth, it is synonymous to the word retainer.

In noting this, a resounding theme of *"...all things work together..."* will perpetuate via experience. This scripture presents the biblical truth that all things experienced at any given time, form allegiances in an effort to yield something good. The spiritual element of work expressed here, parallels the scientific formula for work.

According to the formula, work equals force multiplied by distance (W= F x D). A force or type of weight, multiplies itself by a distance. Distance is sometimes measured in time.

God will, at times, allow weights to multiply themselves for a specific length of time. These weights seemingly work against you, however, they actually work to your advantage.

When the scripture tells us to lay aside the weight that easily besets us, it is also suggesting that there is a weight that does not beset us. The weight that does not beset us becomes an asset for us. How is this, you ask?

The scripture declares, *"a just weight is his delight."* God uses weights to condition or shapes the Body of Christ and to build the arm of the Lord in the life of the believer.

If you initially chose building muscle as the goal of your weight training experience, you will become very acquainted with a variety of weights. It is this same system of weights, properly utilized, that will promote cycles of growth in specific areas.

Muscles experience growth when weight overloads a muscle causing micro trauma and micro tears in the muscle. There is a season, in which, God will allow you to experience a weight of substantial proportion.

It is under a cloud of opposition however that one learns to build muscle. If there is no weighty opposition, there can be no weighty disposition. You may say, I don't necessarily want to build muscle.

I would much rather concentrate on toning up the body. Weights are the instruments that help give the body definition. Even the smallest weight can aid in the process of ridding the body of excess fat.

Before we move any further, I want to caution you; all weight is not healthy weight. Some weight can

7

cause obesity. Your body mass index (BMI) is a good indication of whether or not you are considered healthy.

"BMI is calculated using a comparison of height and weight. At a specific height, a similar weight is considered healthy."

In essence, every spiritual elevation has a similar spiritual weight that is ideal for optimal growth. Just as God uses weights to construct the Body, there are different types of weights the enemy uses for deconstruction and demolition.

Whenever you become tied to something that you have not developed the necessary strength to manage and move, it will manifest in your life as a habit, bondage, or addiction. The pressure that you have no strength or ability to relieve can overpower you, causing you enslavement to it.

There are many different types of weights that only become spiritual holding cells for those who enter in willingly. These weights are only as strong as you make them. Generally, they tend to have little to no power in your life when there is little to no interest at all.

Whenever you begin to give your energy to diabolic weights, they grow gradually in size at small increments. Initially, a weight may only be two pounds.

After one year of feeding that spirit your time and attention, it may now weigh six hundred pounds. It has now become too heavy to move. One-year prior, you had no interest in it at all.

Now, it has become most of what you think about. This weight has not only accessed parts of your brain, but it causes your feelings to have urges and cravings.

Even though a six hundred pound weight would prove to be impossible for most people to move, there is another element that will cause weights to grow at high frequencies. It is called effort…

Feeding diabolic spirits effort or participation, will cause a weight to multiply in size. This is why people in full fellowship with certain things, get hooked faster. They literally can't help it. They've fed all their spiritual strength to a demon, putting their spirit man on life support.

There is however a regimented workout for weights of this magnitude. The Apostle Paul sent a letter to the Galatians highlighting this routine. In chapter five, verse sixteen he tells them to *"WALK."*

Weights that have become immovable will gradually become lighter as you *"Walk in the Spirit."* This very simple action will actually yield the ability to no longer *"...fulfill the lust of the flesh."* Simply put, walking helps you lose weight!!

Maybe you're learning to balance and lift God given weights. You may even be in the process of discarding useless weights. No worries! Both sides work hand in hand to give placement in the spirit. Every time deliverance is experienced, you become postured for elevation.

CHAPTER NOTES:

_____
_____
_____
_____
_____
_____
_____
_____
_____
_____
_____
_____
_____
_____
_____
_____
_____
_____

2

*H*OW MUCH DO I WEIGH?

Ok, *be honest.* You've probably asked yourself a million times, "I wonder how much I weigh?" Well, if you truly desire to reach the correct estimation of your weight, a scale would be the best thing to use. Wondering what a scale is?

It is, simply, an instrument used to measure an object's weight. It also comes in a variety of shapes and sizes. In the vast sport of boxing, weight scales are imperative. They are used to divide boxers into categories known as weight classes. There are seventeen different divisions of weight classes.

These categories range from:

- *Minimum weight (Mini Flyweight)* *105lbs*
- *Light Flyweight (Junior Flyweight)* *108lbs*
- *Flyweight* *112lbs*
- *Super Flyweight (Jr Bantamweight)* *115lbs*
- *Bantamweight* *118lbs*
- *Super Bantamweight (Jr Featherweight)* *122lbs*
- *Featherweight* *126lbs*
- *Super Featherweight (Jr Lightweight)* *130lbs*
- *Lightweight* *135lbs*
- *Super Lightweight (Jr Welterweight)* *140lbs*
- *Welterweight* *147lbs*
- *Super Welterweight (Jr Middleweight)* *154lbs*
- *Middleweight* *160lbs*
- *Super Middleweight* *168lbs*
- *Light Heavyweight* *175lbs*
- *Cruiserweight (Jr Heavyweight)* *200lbs*
- *Heavyweight* .... *>200lbs*

When a fighter weighs in, they're placed into a division based primarily on weight. The weigh in is such an important event.

During this process, fighters are matched with opponents as equally as possible. After the fighter has been properly weighed, they are assigned a weight class.

The boxer now has the official authorization to contend with any fighter within that class. Placing a fighter in an incorrect division can potentially be deadly. This is due to the amount of force someone of a greater body mass could generate.

"Simply put, the bigger the fist, the harder the punch."

In the sport of boxing, every successful boxer has a trainer. The job of a trainer may encompass a small level of teaching however they condition you to execute more proficiently.

"Prophetically, weight class becomes the educational platform that houses teaching and training surrounding your specific level of spiritual capacity."

In weight class, the Lord actually explains more concerning the grace released onto your life for a particular ministry. The curriculum includes everything from assignment to opposition and trial. These are all elements within, what I like to call, the ministry package.

Some of the teaching and training is actually akin to that of on-the-job-training, meaning you get it as you go. As you graduate to upper-level weight classes, the teaching is more intense and the training becomes more rigorous.

The U.S. Army is considered to be one of the most powerful forces in the world due to combat experience, equipment, and TRAINING. This suggests that at minimum, 1/3 of the weight the U.S. Army carries is attributed to the information it has gained. Your knowledge base will only reflect the level of access you've been given.

In first Corinthians, chapter thirteen, Paul validates this theory. In verse eleven he says, *"When I was a child, I spake as a child, I understood as a child, I thought as a child"* because, for a season, Paul's knowledge base reflected that of a child.

This was the highest level of access he had been given. *"But when I became a man, I put away childish things"* due to the new dimension of knowledge that became available as a direct result of increased rank.

The ranking structure for the U.S. Army, highest to lowest, is as follows:

Officers		*Enlisted*	
General of the Army (**Special**)		Sgt Major of the Army (**Special**)	
General	(O-10)	Command Sgt. Major	(E-9)
Lieutenant General	(O-9)	Sergeant Major	(E-9)
Major General	(O-8)	First Sergeant	(E-8)
Brigadier General	(O-7)	Master Sergeant	(E-8)
Colonel	(O-6)	Sergeant First Class	(E-7)
Lieutenant Colonel	(O-5)	Staff Sergeant	(E-6)
Major	(O-4)	Sergeant	(E-5)
Captain	(O-3)	Corporal	(E-4)
First Lieutenant	(O-2)	Specialist	(E-4)
Second Lieutenant	(O-1)	Private First Class	(E-3)
Chief Warrant Officer 5 (W-5)		Private 2	(E-2)
Chief Warrant Officer 4 (W-4)		Private	(E-1)
Chief Warrant Officer 3 (W-3)			
Chief Warrant Officer 2 (W-2)			
Warrant Officer	(W-1)		

This ranking system lists a Private as being the lowest ranked position. The highest achievable rank is the General of the Army.

The General, because of rank, is privy to extremely sensitive information aka (classified). This information will never be made available to a Private due to the low degree of rank.

The President of the United States, being the highest-ranking government official has clearance to the most top-secret information in the world. The American people may never gain even the slightest idea that any of this intel even exists. Why? It's solely due to rank.

In contrast, lets examine a simple visit to the doctor's office. A standard medical checkup begins with the assessment of height and weight. First, the nurse asks you to stand on the scale to measure your weight.

Notice, the same scale is also used while measuring height. After height and weight are calculated, a person can be placed into the corresponding weight group, using the BMI (body mass index). These weight groups are:

Underweight- BMI is < 18.5
Normal weight- BMI is 18.5 – 24.9
Overweight- BMI is 25 – 29.9
Obese- BMI is 30 or >

15

God uses the full "scale" of ministry to articulate rank. Just as natural scales are used to measure weight and height, spiritual scales are also used in this manner.

Spiritually, height represents the degree of spiritual growth one experiences. Height also symbolizes the level of oversight one operates with. Weight represents the capacity one has or how pronounced, in a thing, one is.

The scale of ministry includes the parameter of wisdom, anointing, and opportunity released upon someone for the working of ministry. It also includes the given permissions and authorizations the minister possesses.

In other words, what area of ministry does God allow you to successfully operate in? When you arrive at the correct answer, you will know the "grace" placed on your life for ministry.

"Properly analyzing the scale or dynamics of your ministry will ultimately reveal the rank you occupy."

CHAPTER NOTES:

3

*T*HE WEIGHT OF OIL

Have you ever wondered why some people are better at certain skills and talents than others? Sometimes it even seems as if those individuals are an absolute rarity. In most instances, these occurrences foreshadow an anointing.

The anointing, also known as oil, has two distinct purposes. Isaiah ten and twenty-seven sheds light on the secondary function of the anointing. The Prophet explains, *"... the yoke shall be destroyed because of the anointing."*

THE WEIGHT OF OIL

This scripture attributes a destructive property to the oil that exudes absolute freedom from diabolic weight. The primary function of the anointing, however, is spiritual empowerment. God gives every believer an anointing to accompany his or her ministry assignment.

There is a direct link between anointing and weight. When we revisit Isaiah, the amplified version says, *"...The yoke will be broken because of the fat."* The word fat is synonymous with anointing. As the measure of oil placed upon your life grows, your level of spiritual access changes. A new level of spiritual access demands a new type of spiritual authorization.

Every natural door has a different key assigned to open it. The more secluded and privatized the door or access point, the smaller the number of keys in existence. Having a small amount of keys limits the number of individuals given the ability to open that particular door.

This is what separates lots of individuals. Everyone doesn't have the spiritual permission from God to open certain doors. Whenever God does release a greater level of spiritual authorization to you, it yields a greater spiritual rank.

Enveloped within the full scale of ministry, is the capacity to maintain an *"anointing"*. According to Dr. Paula Price, the anointing, *chrio* in the Greek, gives the necessary components needed to have functionality in ministry.

When applied, the oil unlocks the hidden power and gifting that will enable one to minister. In essence, it is the unction to function. This empowerment "to do" is tied specifically to the Grace released upon your life.

To further our understanding of the oil, consider the 2013 6-series BMW. This car will operate with ease when it receives the necessary amount of motor oil required. Specifically, it requires 6.5 quarts of 5w30 motor oil. These facts help us to arrive at two logical deductions.

The first being, vehicles need a specific amount of oil. Secondly, vehicles need a particular type of oil. In the simplest form, there is, what I like to refer to as, the quality and quantity of oil. In the spirit realm, vehicles symbolize ministry.

So as it pertains to the scale of ministry you have an authorization for, there is a distinct anointing that it requires. Equally, there must also be a sufficient amount of that anointing present to operate in that ministry. As I previously stated, vehicles represent ministry in the spirit realm. Different types of vehicles can symbolize different types of ministry.

For example, *a van is symbolic of family ministry;* while *a tractor-trailer is symbolic of the Church.* It is a fact that the engine in a 2014 Chrysler Town and Country (van) only has the capacity to hold 5.9 quarts of oil.

However, a tractor-trailer can require as many as 60 quarts. When choosing the weight of the oil, there are other factors to take into consideration. Oil weight, or viscosity, refers to how thick or thin the oil is.

If the specified oil meets the Society of Automotive Engineers' (SAE) low requirements, it will display a "W" after the viscosity rating (example: 5w). *The oil that meets the high rating has no letter (example SAE 50).* This code also gives the range by which the oil can be heated and cooled.

The weight of oil required by the van is 5w-20. However, 15w-40 Heavy Duty Diesel and Marine Oil is a weight of oil used in tractor-trailers. This natural explanation of oil gives us a spiritual revelation of the anointing. Just as there are different weights of oil naturally, there are different weights spiritually.

Spiritually, every "vehicle" or ministry has a specific quality and quantity of oil that is necessary for the smooth operation of that ministry. The van or family ministry requires a specific type of anointing.

However, the tractor-trailer or *managing a church* requires an even heavier weight of oil, due to the oil's viscosity. As the engine's temperature grows hot, the oil becomes thinner. If the oil is thicker, it won't burn when introduced to extreme heats.

1 Peter 4:12 tells us to "...*think it not strange concerning the fiery trial which is to try you*." Isn't that interesting?

1 Peter shows us that trials present themselves with fire attached. So when your ministry is under fire, having the proper weight of oil is the assurance the trial won't burn you alive. Without the recommended oil, you don't have the authorization to win at that weight class.

In other words, if you bear the anointing of an Evangelist, you will lose the warfare that comes for the anointing associated with an Apostle. If you are not a Prophet but call yourself one, the demons that bring a war to Prophets, will fight you unnecessarily.

Not only does different ministries require different anointings, but they also need different amounts of that oil to flow efficiently.

Whenever you check the oil in your car, the dipstick typically displays a minimum to maximum indicator. Just as there is a minimum amount of oil needed to operate your vehicle, there is a minimum required to function spiritually in any given ministry. Ask God, specifically, what area of ministry He has graced you with.

When you know that, you will be most effective. If you are facilitating an area in ministry you don't possess an anointing for, you don't have the grace to succeed there. What happens when you don't have an anointing?

"Did you know that if there is no motor oil in your car, the motor will lock-up, leaving the vehicle inoperable and immobile?"

Think about your spiritual vehicle. If you do not have the anointing for a particular ministry, there can be no operation nor progression. The full weight of anointing encompasses information. It does not just only speak of power, but it is also a partnership of knowledge.

1 John 2:27 says, *"the same anointing teacheth you of all things."* The scripture suggests to me that the

empowerment I have received can also instruct me, just as a teacher teaches a class.

We all know David's story... David was anointed on three different occasions before he became the King. There was a span of approximately fifteen years between the first and last anointing.

Within those fifteen years, David was able to gain useful information concerning the Kingship. He even learned lessons spanning from the topic of marriage to war.

Working for King Saul enabled David to not only receive information but training as well. All these lessons and more were a required training to be a successful ruler.

CHAPTER NOTES:

4

CARRYING EXTRA WEIGHT

Certain foods will cause even more of an increase in weight than others. Some people choose to eat simply because food is available, however others decide to eat because they feel the urge or need to grow or feed something within.

For this reason pregnant women eat multiple times per day. The female, over a period of nine months, undergoes a drastic change in weight. This increase in weight happens daily as the woman feeds the baby she carries as well as herself.

As she feeds, the shape of her body will stretch from normal to what's considered extreme. More of the times, the size they've become is the largest they've ever been. There are two factors that will regulate a pregnant mother's appetite.

Based on the size of the baby, her appetite may grow larger in comparison to that of someone carrying a smaller baby. The bigger baby will yield a greater need for food than the smaller. The quantity of babies will also govern a mother's appetite.

What's interesting is, *psych* is a Greek word for the mind. It makes reference to the soul. The soul deals with the part of you that has desires or an appetite.

"This is powerful when we considered that, spiritually, women symbolize the church and her appetite only consists of the Word of God."

More specifically the word is classified in scripture as milk and meat. In the sixth chapter of John, even Jesus announces himself as the "bread" of life. As I fore stated, the woman, being a typology for the church, has an appetite that grows as a result of what she carries.

A baby is spiritually symbolic of something new.

What I carry is reflected in my appetite for God and His word. Depending upon how much I carry, eating may be even more of a dire need for some than others.

The second verse of Romans chapter twelve challenges the believer to *"...be ye transformed by the renewing of your mind..."*. The Greek word for transformed is *metamorpho*. It means to change into another form.

Mind, or *nous* is the Greek word deals with perceiving and understanding. Through science we have learned that the brain is the central processing unit for the natural body.

Simply put, it understands natural things. The mind, however, speaks to a spiritual faculty within that has an ability to comprehend spiritually.

When we revisit the text, it now reveals something slightly different to the "Body" of Christ at large. Paul says that the body should allow itself to change into another form by the continual process of perceiving and understanding.

In essence, the "Body" of Christ will display visible change based solely around the information or word the mind eats. This change is commonly known as gaining weight.

A pregnant mother will continue to gain weight through out the process of child bearing. The word that she takes in is what supplies the new thing, within her womb, the necessary nutrients to give birth to a healthy baby. The mother not only experiences growth in stomach size, but also her feet will swell to a new size.

"The spiritual significance of feet is movement in ministry."

This implies that when God births something new out of me, He then increases the rank of my ministry. If we look more closely at the rank gained by way of capacity, we are introduced to a term known as "deadweight tonnage."

Deadweight tonnage measures a ship's capacity to safely carry weight. More specifically, it calculates the total weight of things like cargo, fuel, passengers and crew. The weight of the ship is however excluded. Another name for a ship is vessel.

Spiritually, you become that vessel that has the ability to carry. The measure of a vessel's capacity will outline how much weight it can carry. This will not include the weight of the vessel itself though.

Moreover, from capacity alone, you can derive at a

pretty close estimation as to the nature of the vessel's rank. It's a very elementary concept. Small boats have small capacities but larger vessels have larger capacities.

CHAPTER NOTES:

5

*F*OLLOWING THE LITER

Not everyone gains a noticeable amount of weight just by consuming food alone. Rather, some increase their weight based upon the liquids they choose to drink. In Hebrews the tenth chapter, seventh verse, Jesus says, *"Lo, I come (in the volume of the book...)."*

When Jesus used the word volume, he was referencing a scientific term. Science teaches that volume is three-dimensional space occupied by a gas, liquid or solid. It is measured in cubic units, such as liters, cubic meters, gallons and ounces.

The full measure of volume is calculated in, what science calls, a liter. The measurement by which you can calculate potential spiritual weight is called a Leader.

"In other words, you can look at the anointing your leader walks in and that will give you an idea of the weight you will potentially carry."

There are lots of people that serve under great leadership, all the while expecting to receive of their anointing. These individuals also seek ways to esteem their leaders through the fulfillment of duties and assignments.

Although admirable, these things do not always guarantee that the anointing on your leader will rest on you. The weight of leadership can only be accessed when you, the disciple, permit yourself to be poured into.

After this permission has been given, you must maintain a close connection to leadership. This theory makes perfect since when we parallel it with a natural example.

Let's just say, I am thirsty and desire water from a pitcher. The pitcher is symbolic of your leader. A glass would be representative of you. You are an empty vessel waiting and desiring to be poured into.

Let me caution you though. As leadership begins to pour into you, stay close! This is a very critical concept. If the vessel is not positioned close enough to the pitcher, substance may be wasted as well as time. Pouring into a vessel becomes a smoother transaction when he or she follows the leader very closely.

After a son or daughter is poured into, they now have the ability to do all that their spiritual parent does. Jesus was a leader that had a core of twelve disciples.

He assured them in the book of John, the fourteenth chapter and the twelfth verse, that "*He that believeth on me, the works that I do shall he do also.*"

This is the assuring guarantee that even if you don't progress into new spiritual territory, you at-least possess the same abilities your leader possesses. If properly connected to your leader, what has become their ceiling in ministry then becomes your floor.

35

You can stand on the height of their ministry and build from there. John the fourteen chapter and verse twelve, gives the written validation for this theory. Jesus said not only will you accomplish what I've accomplished, but *"Greater [works] than these shall he do."* This declaration was filled with spiritual implication.

As a leader, Jesus possessed the authorization or key to unlock a greater level of capacity in the lives of those that followed him. When Jesus makes this announcement, it's symbolic of a key being placed into a locked door and turned.

Now the disciples had gained access to space or capacity that was never made available prior to this episode. Although the capacity of the disciples grew their rank had not as of yet.

The opening of new capacity only spoke to the potential weight they stood to gain. As the disciples later begin to operate in the grace released upon their lives, their capacity began to fill and even expand. This is the point where the disciples actually increased in rank.

Before anyone increases in rank, their current capacity must be completely filled. When there is no longer any space to occupy, you need new space. For example, lets say you symbolize a one-liter bottle.

Then you allow someone to pour substance into your life, completely filling you to the brim. Now you have reached full capacity. You have no additional space to receive anything.

Not another drop can be poured into your life until the container has been upgraded. You may have started with a one-liter Mountain Dew bottle but because your capacity was filled, your rank actually increased. Now your rank changed to that of a two-liter Mountain Dew bottle.

When it comes to understanding rank, there is a perpetual cycle that spiritual ranking systems use. This cycle says that a full capacity will automatically introduce a new rank. However, a new rank will always release a new capacity.

The disciples saw this first hand. After Jesus released His capacity to them, they filled it. By filling it they then increased they're rank thus tapping into the "greater works" clause of scripture. Now they had a new rank that released a new capacity for God!

CHAPTER NOTES:

_____
_____
_____
_____
_____
_____
_____
_____
_____
_____
_____
_____
_____
_____
_____
_____
_____
_____
_____
_____
_____
_____
_____
_____
_____

6

$\mathcal{W}$EIGHT OF OPPOSITION

You may be wondering, "What can I do to exercise my UPPER body effectively?" Excellent question. The answer is very simple.

All you need is a little weight!!!

As you apply weight to your body, the state of your body will begin to change. As you continue to utilize the weight, your natural body will progressively show results. The phrase "upper body," used in this discussion, is indicative of your spiritual body. Your spirit gets the most efficient workout when it learns to use weights properly.

The Apostle Paul was a very educated man as well as a noted spiritual authority in the Kingdom. Through his writings, many mysteries and truths were unlocked. One such truth was mentioned briefly in his letter to the Philippian believers.

In chapter three, verse fourteen he wrote, *"I press toward the mark for the prize of the high calling of God in Christ Jesus."* Let's look a little closer within this verse. Apostle Paul says to the reader, "I press."

Let's further analyze the verb "press - to act upon with steadily applied weight or force." We can then use logical reasoning to understand better that if Paul was pressing against something, there was more than likely something pressing against him.

The science behind this press would be suggestive of what is known as g-force. G-force is the measurement of the type of acceleration that causes weight. This kind of acceleration is produced when the surfaces of two objects are pushed against each other. The reaction-force of this push yields an equal and opposite weight for every unit of the objects' mass.

Basically, an invisible force called gravity pushes against any object that initiates acceleration, causing weight. Answer this question. To what does gravity bare a high similarity? Consider that gravity is an invisible force that operates within the earth's atmosphere.

Ephesians 2:2 talks about *"the prince of the power of the air."* The prince is the spiritual force of opposition that works against Godly progression; his weapon of choice used to bring resistance is weight.

G-force also teaches us that a plane engaging in a straight and level flight, uses this formula lifting equal weight (L=W). When the plane shifts into a sloping turn of 60 degrees, the pilot experiences 2 g and weight doubles. The equation now reads L=2W.

The steeper the angle of the turn, the greater the G-force an object will undergo. Not only does the enemy fight against my forward progression, but the weight of opposition doubles as I turn away from people, places and things that aren't good for me.

God told his people in Chronicles 7:14 to *"turn from their wicked ways."* Turning was the completion of a process that resulted in God speaking, forgiving, and healing.

41

Ezekiel 33 also promotes the turn by cautioning the wicked to *"turn from his way and live"* (verse 11). It is my belief that the enemy doubles the weight of a turn in an attempt to keep us bound; which is why it is so hard for some people to repent. The word, repent or *(metanoe)* in the Greek means to have a change of mind. It involves a turning with remorse from sin to God.

Paul further explains this theory in Romans 7:21-23, when he says, "*I find then a law, that when I would do good, evil is present with me. For I delight in the law of God after the inward man: But I see another law in my members, warring against the law of my mind."*

These verses highlight a spiritual law that is directly related to the resistance incurred by turning. As we consistently strive for Godly perfection, according to spiritual law, there is a force of evil that will strive against every believer.

"The enemy does not necessarily have intentions to take you down, but rather to weight you down."

He does not want you to move forward or go higher. He has already made an approximate calculation as to the level of success God has released over your life. When you consider this, you will understand why the enemy wants you at a stand still. If

Satan ever allowed you to excel or accelerate in God, he knows centripetal force would govern your life.

Centripetal force acts on your body in a curved path by forcing you to continue on that way. The enemy is banking on this approximation.

"If he can weight you down early in the game, he feels that he can stop a season of continued blessing and success."

CHAPTER NOTES:

_____

_____

_____

_____

_____

_____

_____

_____

_____

_____

_____

_____

_____

_____

_____

_____

_____

_____

_____

_____

_____

_____

_____

_____

7

STRENGTH TRAINING

As we migrate to the subject of strength training, you will discover that the body's degree of strength is inevitably connected to its degree of weakness. The scripture found in 2 Corinthians 12:10, shares a very powerful truth. It assures us that *"when I am weak, then am I strong."*

Here is where the opportunity for substitution presents itself. This spiritual law grants permission to substitute weakness of any kind, for strength of every kind. It speaks to an absolute state of strength that has

45

no degree of inaccurate execution. This limitless spectrum of strength is only apparent because it is divine in nature. The origin of this strength was enveloped within the concept of *"wait training."*

The totality of what "*weight training*" is, includes what "*wait training*" does. The twenty-seventh chapter of Psalms tells us to *"wait on the LORD: be of good courage, and he shall strengthen thine heart: wait, I say, on the LORD."* From this text, we discover that strength originates from a place of waiting.

Isaiah 40:31 - exclaimed, through prophetic dissertation, that those who choose to *"wait upon the LORD shall renew their strength."* The Hebrew word for renew is (*chalaph*). It means *to change for the better*. This word implies that strength can be changed to a better state.

For example, a weightlifter decides to bench-press 250lbs ten times (reps). After he executes a total of twenty reps, he chooses to pause for a breather. Just before attempting another set of reps, he increases the weight to 260lbs and repeats the process.

Between the weight increase, there was a brief pause. After this moment of waiting, the weightlifter experiences a regeneration of strength. Now he can lift a greater degree of weight because he waited.

Another example of "*wait training*", is seen in the Upper-Room. Jesus told the disciples, "*I will send you the one my Father has promised, but you must STAY in the city until you are given power from heaven*" (*John 24:49*)

"A procession of waiting was succeeded by power."

Seasons of waiting come to renew your spiritual strength. God has ordained these seasons to equip you with the ability to push against the opposition in stronger weight classes successfully. According to the dictionary, strength is: "*the quality or state of being strong as well as having bodily, muscular, and mental power.*"

The definition shows us that strength is synonymous with muscular and mental power. This sheds light on the phrase coined by Sir Francis Bacon, "*Knowledge is power.*"

Through this phrase, Bacon suggests that without any aid, knowledge is the very same thing as power. Power, here, could be equated to that of a shotgun that fires shells as well as the force created when two vehicles collide.

"Knowledge is no different. It can potentially be just as constructive or deconstructive."

Proverbs 24:5 says *"A wise man is strong; yea, a man of knowledge increaseth strength."*

If a man is counted wise, this suggests that he has acquired a great deal of knowledge. When someone is considered knowledgeable, it is because they've gathered a significant amount of information.

Consider Proverbs 24:5, It reveals that a person, who has gathered a great deal of knowledge, is wise. Not only are you wise, but you are also strong. The second clause of the scripture tells us that as we repetitiously acquire or perform reps of knowledge, we get stronger.

Why is this type of strength training so important? The enemy wages war and attacks you in your soulish realm. Wondering where your soulish realm is located?

Over the years, movies have caused me to believe that my soul was located in my stomach. You may have even been thinking the same thing. However, your soul, from the Greek *psych,* is the seat of the feelings, desires, affections and aversions.

More specifically, the soul is a two-part entity comprised of the heart and mind. James 1:21 says *"receive and welcome the Word which implanted and*

48

rooted [in your hearts] contains the power to save your souls."

He is saying that there is a particular type of knowledge that includes a power to, in turn, protect our minds; which is why the enemy fights us so strong in our minds. He is trying to claim it as his territory. The Word of God is your POWER. Use it!

There is a matching level of word knowledge that parallels each level of demonic attack. The stronger the attack, the more of God's word you will need to combat the enemy.

The more of God's word you know, the stronger you become. As your word knowledge increases, your spiritual weight increases also.

Just as a child is ranked at a second grade level academically, it is equally possible to be ranked at a second grade level spiritually. The academic ranking system is based largely on the comprehension of required information.

Although there are several prerequisites for academic advancement, the greatest centers on information. After receiving and retaining the required information, the student automatically experiences something called graduation. Spiritually, the ministry anointing assigned to developing children is the trainer.

Just as a school-age child is required to retain given information, God requires his children to retain pertinent information. This invaluable information is known as the word of God. As you feed yourself God's word, your spirit receives the proper nutrients to grow.

As you increase in word knowledge, which yields fresh revelation, your spirit will continue to gain weight. This never-ending process of gaining weight will ultimately increase your spiritual rank.

Proverbs 24:10 says *"if you faint in the day of adversity, your strength is small."*

From this, we can gain a scale to measure strength. The *"day of adversity"* includes adverse conditions as well as the adversary, himself. If he or any situation causes you to give up, you are not counted as being weak, but rather as possessing a low level of strength.

It's like having the strength of a toddler to push a wheel barrel full of cement. The only time the enemy, of our soul, can win is when you don't have the knowledge of God's word. There may even be times where you feel as though *"my flesh and my heart faileth"* (Psalm 73:26).

As a result of having received the word of the Lord willingly, *"God [is] then the strength of my heart"* (Psalm 73:26). After I receive the word of God, I now have the knowledge, which manifests as the strength needed to protect my heart, as well as my mind.

One of the many advantages to "wait training" is the fact that it strengthens your wait. The new level of strength, alone, is very rewarding. There are however a few more advantages that follow the posture of waiting.

"But they that wait upon the Lord shall renew [their] strength; they shall mount up with wings as eagles; they shall run, and not be weary; [and] they shall walk, and not faint." (Isaiah 40:31)

Maintaining your "wait" properly will reciprocate a healthier lifestyle. Firstly, it causes us to have *"wings as eagles;"* which is a lighter more uplifted feeling. Things like depression and the spirit of heaviness have no authority.

When the scripture speaks of running and not being in a state of weariness, it is referencing perseverance. It also deals with progressing at a faster than normal rate. Although oxymoronic, waiting and moving forward are prophetically synonymous. The Prophet Isaiah made his last prophetic implication saying, *"they shall walk and not faint."*

51

This statement suggests that even on a basic level of production, there will be advancement at a consistent pace. The type of progression mentioned here, will not cause a sluggish or tired feeling but rather it will yield a determination to finish.

CHAPTER NOTES:

_____

_____

_____

_____

_____

_____

_____

_____

_____

_____

_____

_____

_____

_____

_____

_____

_____

_____

8

*W*E WEIGH MORE TOGETHER

Have you ever utilized a public elevator? Flown on an airplane? Surely you've ridden the yellow school bus at least once as a child. You're probably wondering what each of these have in common? The common denominator is that they are all modes of transportation designed to carry multiple people per trip, just like the church!

If you said yes to elevators, consider this. Public elevators often display signs that alert the users of the capacity limit. A standard elevator's capacity generally ranges between 1,000 and 6,000 pounds. Typically, elevators in small residential buildings have lower capacity limits because they ascend no more than four or five floors.

The Apostle Paul cautions believers not to engage in the practice of "*forsaking the assembling of ourselves together*" (Hebrews 10:25).

When we assemble ourselves together, there is a specific type of weight that is released amidst a family of believers. Scientifically speaking, weight is the force exerted on mass by a gravitational field. Mass is the property which reflects the quantity of matter within a sample.

Although related, weight and mass are distinctly different. However, the formula for weight (W=mg), suggests though different, the weight of an object is directly linked to its mass.

When analyzing this equation spiritually, I began to spark with illumination when considering the need for fellowship. For instance, let's consider the denomination of Catholicism; which envelops a variety of ways, in which the parishioners worship God. Note the significance of the name for the central act of corporate worship; it is known as *"Mass"*. Now, this is where we pull revelation...

In order to have weight, there must be *Mass*. The more mass a body has, ultimately the more weight it has. As the Body of Christ grows in body mass, our weight of influence in the earth realm grows.

The Body of Christ is ideally purposed to weigh on the world's scale; depending on its mass, and can be permitted to weigh in on political, economic and governmental issues.

Collectively, the Body of Christ has the ability to apply the weight of God's will within every social arena we have influence in. We are more effective weighing in together in times of crisis, than by attempting to individually. Spiritual rank increases progressively when we operate in unity.

Lets take a spiritually observation of elevators again. There may be ten people on an elevator that weigh a total of 1,500 pounds. Lets take into account that you weigh 150 pounds. Alone you only weigh a fraction of everyone's combined weight. The minute you step onto the elevator, however, a few things will transpire.

First, your individual capacity will shift to collective capacity. Collective capacity, in turn, unveils the true magnitude of the new space. It was much easier to calculate your individual capacity initially but at this point, everything merges.

After collective capacity is created, the total weight increases tremendously. Being that this elevator has a smaller capacity limit, it falls under the category of elevators that only ascend to low levels.

Prophetically, this suggests that gatherings of people with small capacities are never equipped to experience high levels of advancement. Simply put, small-minded individuals don't have the capability the think high.

Elevators found in tall structures such as skyscrapers, operate a little differently. They have a much larger capacity limit than those found in smaller buildings. Implying, that in larger gatherings you gain a much greater capacity to receive, based on the rank of the atmospheric weight pull.

Amongst a greater capacity to unify with others, gives the leverage for my mind to configure new levels of thinking. Iron sharpens iron... ***Proverbs 27:17***

In other words, the greater the capacity, the greater the progression that is made available to a gathering. Progression exists to bring advancement. It consists of things like strategies and fresh ideas. This is why businesses gather partners via meetings with the intent to gain new perspective on company endeavors. It is within this cycle where perpetual progression warrants access to new levels of spiritual rank.

In contrast, a dead man is generally thought to carry more weight than a living one. People worldwide have accepted this idea as absolute truth. However, this idea is not true at all. A dead body maintains the same weight as that of a living body.

I'm sure this sounds perplexing, but consider that a live body can give assistance in lifting itself, where a non-living body cannot. A live body can distribute its weight, which changes the gravitational center.

On the other hand, a load of dead weight will form its center of gravity around the area being supported. The load itself will not give any assistance. This is what causes the load to seem as if it gained more weight. All the weight is directing itself one way causing the load to only feel heavier. In all actuality, the load's weight never changed.

In 1st Corinthians 15:31, Paul introduces a new exercise to add to your daily workout. In the second clause of that verse he says that, *"I die daily."* Paul was on a life long mission to kill carnality in his life. Each day he allowed some aspect of who he was to die. Paul understood something very powerful.

The full weight of God's power would never be experienced in his ministry, had his life not yielded dead weight. I believe that fleshy death occurred every time Paul allowed God to direct and instruct him.

When God becomes the center of your focus, you no longer desire to "throw your weight around." Your selfish desires die every time you starve your flesh with Godly obedience.

Whenever you train yourself to die daily, death actually becomes the key that unlocks capacity. After capacity is unlocked, the stage has now become set to handle more weight. As I fore stated, a dead man does not grow in weight but rather his capacity is opened to receive the full weightiness of God.

When Jesus died, his capacity was enlarged beyond anything He had ever experienced on earth. Death operated as a gateway for ascension to a rank that had never been earthly achievable.

It was the pre-qualification needed to step up to the next place spiritually. This new rank was literally "out of this world." According to Philippians chapter two, verse nine; God *"highly exalted him."* This is where God officially released new rank to Jesus.

Along with this new promotion, the scripture proceeds by giving more insight into His new position. It says that Jesus was given *"a name which is above every name."*

Jesus now outranked everyone and everything making Him only second to God. Verse 10 gives the reader perspective into the degree of prestige woven into His promotion. This new rank encompassed such a level of honor it now required *"that at the name of Jesus every knee should bow."*

The scripture continues to unfold by explaining the boundaries of jurisdictional authorization given to Jesus. This new office allowed Him to govern *"... things in heaven, and things in earth, and things under the earth."*

After Jesus received His heavenly installment, there had to be an earthly reception. This is why verse eleven presents the inevitable truth that *"every tongue should confess that Jesus Christ is Lord."* This amendment would establish Jesus as Lord, in the earth.

The result of properly establishing His governmental authority in the earth, would be the global recognition that *"...***the government shall be upon his shoulder...***"* It goes back to the rank of jurisdictional authority Jesus had been given.

CHAPTER NOTES:

9

*W*EIGHT OF OPPORTUNITY

In the book of Numbers, chapter thirteen, we gain a fresh perspective. The Israelites had just come out of an old season in Egypt and were embarking on a new season of promise in Canaan. God told Moses to send twelve different men out to observe the demographics of the land.

Upon careful observation, these men were to report in detail concerning the people and cities therein; this report would include things such as competition in business, housing markets, and the land appraisal.

Within the report, the men were also instructed, in verse twenty, to bring back intelligence concerning *"the land... whether it [be] fat or lean."* They were to evaluate the land in an attempt to approximate the total weight of this new opportunity.

As it relates to spiritual capacity, Israel carried a promise for hundreds of years. That promise was spoken from the highest-ranking official of all-time, God. His rank alone establishes his word as truth because **He cannot lie**. His rank also guarantees that His word can never be voided out but will accomplish and prosper wherever He sends it.

Of course, there were a few different assessments that were brought back. There was also an evil report given in an effort to hinder God's people from advancing.

It was, however, imperative that Israel made progress, so God gave his people an incentive. Grapes!!! The grapes were a prophetic declaration from God to the people, concerning their next season. During this season, they would experience an extreme level of fruitfulness. Fruit is the manifestation of a seed.

In Genesis 22:17, God told Abraham *"in multiplying I will multiply thy seed as the stars of the heaven, and as the sand which is upon the sea shore."*

By way of that prophetic word, the children of Israel were now in a season where they had an over-abundance of seed. If there is an over-abundance of a particular seed, there will inevitably be an over-abundant harvest.

These grapes were gigantic in size! The grapes' size was also a visual representation of the degree of fruitfulness the season would produce. That's why grapes are considered "produce."

Grapes were used to make wine. The wine was typically served at weddings, and scripturally, earmarks celebration. Had Israel accurately calculated the weight of the opportunity, grapes would've suggested that the coming season was celebration worthy.

It all began with a seed. First the seed was planted and established in the earth. Then the seed was multiplied several times over and over and over. Abraham's seed multiplied exponentially, constantly yielding new capacity.

The more the seed was multiplied, the more the Israelites' capacity grew. This provides insight as to why the older generation walked in the wilderness for so long.

That generation was so rebellious and hardheaded; Although Israel's capacity was open, they never grew their capacity to the degree needed to receive opportunity from God. They asked God for things yet lacked developed capacity to receive opportunity.

This is why they kept having conversations about returning to Egypt, the place of NO opportunity. In a forty-year span, the Israelites never experienced real progression. There was a land, in which, God had ordained a steady rate of advancement for His people.

Sadly most of the older generation never partook of it. Hence the reason the younger generation went into the promise land. They were able to embrace the fullness of the opportunity God had placed in their laps.

Proverbs 18:16 says, *"A man's gift maketh room for him, and bringeth him before great men."* The word "gift" in this scripture makes reference to something tangible. It speaks more of an offering. Based upon the offering, one would gain an opportunity to come into an environment filled with VIPs.

There is however a dichotomy to this scripture. The gift being spoken of here also refers to whatever gifting God has given you to operate in.

The Easy To Read Version Bible, gives a new perspective of Proverbs by suggesting that, *"Gifts can open many doors..."* Your gift or seed is the actual key that unlocks doors. What doors? Doors that have the ability to house opportunities that will *"help you meet important people."*

The capacity that allows you to receive opportunity is reflected in the size of your gifting. The greater the gift becomes, the greater the authorization to receive becomes. Your gift is what assists you in ministry. It is also one of a few helpful elements that are engrafted into the full scale of your ministry. A specific rank merits a level of opportunity that, in turn, requires a corresponding gifting.

According to scripture, *"A man's gift"* will build a *"room for him..."* to occupy. It's almost as if your gift, literally, grows hands and feet to stand and construct the room that houses the opportunity. The opportunity that lives in the room is never larger than the room built by the gift.

An opportunity will never present itself outside of the level of manageability your gift possesses. This is the reason gifts and opportunities unfold on corresponding levels at different degrees of spiritual rank.

CHAPTER NOTES:

_____

_____

_____

_____

_____

_____

_____

_____

_____

_____

_____

_____

_____

_____

_____

_____

_____

_____

_____

_____

_____

10

*T*HE WEIGHT RELATIONSHIP CARRIES

Relationships come in different shapes and sizes. When you evaluate the purpose of a particular relationship, you must consider the weight of the relationship.

The bible lets us know that, *"While He was still talking to the crowds, it happened that His mother and brothers stood outside, asking to speak to Him. Someone said to Him, Look! Your mother and Your brothers are standing outside asking to speak to You."*

67

Jesus replied to the one who told Him, "Who is My mother and who are My brothers?" And stretching out His hand toward His disciples [and all His other followers], He said, "Here are My mother and My brothers! For whoever does the will of My Father who is in heaven [by believing in Me, and following Me] is My brother and sister and mother." (Matthew 12:46-50)

In these verses, 46-50, Jesus gives us a hard pill to swallow. He shows us that spiritual connection with God outweighs the most highly esteemed of earthly relationships, including that of a son and mother. I believe he chose to convey this truth because there will always be people that can relate to family.

A large percentage of people are bound to their family's opinion of what their career, spouse, geographical location, religion and even political preference should be; because of familiar spirits, lots of times, relationships, such as family, can form ungodly attachments.

Let's look towards the greatest example, Jesus. There was a wedding in the second chapter of John. Jesus and His Mom, Mary, were in attendance. After all the wine was gone, Mary says to her son, *"They don't have any more wine.*" Jesus replied, "*Mother, why do you involve me? My time has not yet come.*"

Here we encounter Mary giving Jesus the heads-up about the wine shortage. She simply tells Her son, "They ran out." Jesus replies by saying, "Mom, not yet. Its not yet time for me to operate with that type of weight just yet."

Jesus's response implies that Mary was awaiting a specific action. Although Mary makes no verbal request, it is apparent that she has an expectation. Her expectation is derived from the idea that the weight of her relationship with Jesus would be the key to initiating a miracle.

John chapter eleven also displays the weight of relationship. Consider Lazarus; the storyline reads, "*Now a certain [man] was sick, [named] Lazarus... Therefore his sisters sent unto him, saying, Lord, behold, he whom thou lovest is sick.*"

The text immediately reveals the nature of Jesus's relationship with Lazarus. Jesus even told the disciples, "*...Our friend Lazarus sleepeth.*" Not only does Jesus love Lazarus, He considers him a friend. The scriptures also record Jesus weeping for His friend Lazarus.

69

THE WEIGHT RELATIONSHIP CARRIES

Of course, by this time Lazarus was dead... When Jesus comes to pay His respects he has two conversations with Martha and Mary of Bethany, Lazarus's sisters. They were upset with Jesus because He chose to take His time getting there.

During an emotional conversation with Mary of Bethany, the scripture says, "**When Jesus, therefore, saw her weeping, and the Jews also weeping which came with her, he groaned in the spirit, and was troubled.**"

This story displays an adamant weight of relationship. The strength was so great, it guaranteed Lazarus a miracle that not even, rigor mortis could restrict.

The weight of relationship is extremely important to God. It's so important until God has deemed it to be the prerequisite by which one gains entrance into Heaven. Jesus was teaching in the book of Luke, the thirteenth chapter, when he was asked a question. The question was, "...**Lord, are there few that be saved?**"

Jesus gave an answer that was full of insight. He said, "**Do all you can to go in by the narrow door! A lot of people will try to get in, but will not be able to.**" He even told them their conversation would be,

"We dined with you, and you taught in our streets."
But he will say, "I really don't know who you are!"

This is so powerful because we live in a world where most people are only conscious of their relationship with God. This explains why so many people are quick to recite, "I know God" as a defensive tactic. Although this statement may have a degree of truth attached to it, I wonder how many people have considered whether or not God knows them.

Jesus is simply saying, at the conclusion of this life, he will evaluate the weight of His relationship with the individual, not the individual's relationship with him. This is why He said, "*I know you not.*"

It's not that the individual wouldn't know about Him, but rather He doesn't know them. He never developed an authentic relationship with that person in all areas, including total obedience.

Morever, it makes sense when you consider the people that say they know you. They may know everything there is to know about you. They may even know your darkest secrets. Even with all of that knowledge, you may never have even met this person. This happens to celebrities all the time.

People form all sorts of imaginary relationships with movie stars and musicians they've never met.

Some fans even claim to be involved in serious relationships with these celebrities – which are called groupies. Although the fan has developed some sort of relationship with the celebrity, the celebrity has no idea the person even exists.

I'm reminded of a powerful word the Lord ministered to me a few years ago. He said, *"Even a tree will grow away from its roots in order to be fruitful."* There is a heightened experience that one will gain away from roots stemming from areas such as your heritage, birthplace, and foundational church that will produce seasons of fruitfulness.

True success does not exist where there is limited perspective and no exposure. In fact, truly being successful does not occur until you push away from relationships that aren't God inspired and push towards a greater relationship with God. As we grow our spiritual relationship, subsequent relationships will either grow, due to the spirit of God or collapse, due to carnality.

As Christian believers, we must always evaluate the weight of relationship. Is that relationship birthed out of carnality, which will promote a type of bondage? Or is the Father the mutual connector, inspiring righteousness?

The weight of relationship also implies a degree of strength that each relationship carries. Just as bridges have max load capacities, every relationship contains a maximum limit of pressure it can withstand before collapsing.

Let's continue with our discussion of relationships amongst the area of family. I'm sure there are many different scenarios we could explore, but I'm only going to review just a few. Moses's relationship with his sister, Miriam, was put to the test. Miriam didn't agree with Moses's choice for a wife, so she talked trash about her. This ultimately caused leprosy to fall on Miriam.

Eli, the priest, had two sons that were also priests named Hophni and Phinehas. These young men were very irreverent. They misused their sacred priestly office to be unholy and carnal. They did everything from sleeping with temple women to taking larger portions of the offering than permitted. Due to the nature of their relationship, Eli never addressed the issues.

David, Jesse's son, experienced a long season of rejection with his family. That same rejection caused him to quit the family owned business of working with sheep.

This spirit was also influential in David's decision to accept a new job working for somebody that didn't like him just to get away from his family. Those are just a few examples. You may be asking yourself what the load capacity of your relationship with God is.

1 Peter 5:7, tells us to remain in a continual state of *"Casting the whole of your care [all your anxieties, all your worries, all your concerns, once and for all] on Him, for He cares for you affectionately and cares about you watchfully."*

That scripture gives me the assurance that there is a limitless capacity of weight my relationship with God can handle.

It will NEVER collapse under pressure.

Now consider God's relationship with you. Psalms 69:19 speaks to the load capacity of this bridge when it says the Lord *"daily loadeth us with benefits."*

A daily load suggests that God gives us only what we can handle every day. If He gave us all the benefits at one time, the extra weight could alter the motive for having relationship with God. In other words, God allows us to benefit from relationships at smaller increments to keep the nature of our relationship with Him pure.

CHAPTER NOTES:

_____

_____

_____

_____

_____

_____

_____

_____

_____

_____

_____

_____

_____

_____

_____

_____

_____

_____

_____

_____

_____

_____

11

I AM THE WAY

Jesus said, "*I am the way*" in John 14:6. This gives us a perspective on direction. Know this. You cannot way (weigh) yourself. If you feel you can, consider what wisdom teaches us in Proverbs 14:12, "*There is a way which seemeth right unto a man, but the end thereof are the ways of death.*"

Here we clearly see that man has his way of choosing what seems to be the better path for his life. Proverbs 16:9 clearly resounds this theory whereas *"A man's mind plans his way [as he journeys through life],*

But the Lord directs his steps and establishes them."
The word "way", speaks of direction and is
synonymous with directives, and instructions. This
scripture suggests that without any thought, God will
direct each step you take, follow or implement.

However, your carnal mind will formulate a plan
or strategy it deems appropriate for the life you
envision. For this reason, God said, *"I know the
thoughts that I think toward you... to give you an
expected end (Jeremiah 29:11)."*

"God has already taken the guesswork out of your life."

A believer no longer has to make decisions
utilizing trial and error. God has already plotted your
life's course. Ask yourself a question. How many times,
per day, do I make decisions without consulting God?

2 Corinthians 10:4-5 says, "*(For the weapons of
our warfare are not carnal, but mighty through God to
the pulling down of strong holds;) Casting down
imaginations, and every high thing that exalteth itself
against the knowledge of God.*"

The Apostle Paul is teaching a quick overview of
spiritual warfare. He tells us to pull down strongholds
and cast down imaginations and high things that exalt

themselves against knowledge. It's imperative to know that. All the enemy is fighting is knowledge. We've already discovered that the full weight of oil encompasses information.

Proverbs 3:5-6 cautions us to *"lean not unto thine own understanding"* but *"In all thy ways acknowledge him, and he shall direct thy paths."*

The fullness of who God called you to be is connected to where he told you to go. The Prophet, Moses, understood this philosophy in full detail after he left the desert.

God told Moses to go back to Egypt and release the prophetic word of the Lord into an oppressive atmosphere. Even though Moses understood the assignment in the desert, it was not until he was back in Egypt that the full measure of who he was could be seen.

Before Moses knew his true identity and began walking in the way of God's instruction, he first had to acknowledge God. Acknowledgment is the tool by which the Lord ways or directs you.

"If the enemy can trick you into not acknowledging God, you will lack direction that yields identity."

Notice, the word acknowledge bears a strong likeness to the spelling of the word knowledge. Prophetically, *acknowledge* becomes a type of *knowledge*. It is the knowledge you act upon; because we understand the enemy is fighting knowledge, we must also understand he is fighting our willingness to acknowledge as well.

After Moses develops a knowledge base for God, he is then able to act upon the knowledge he receives. This development takes place during the episode of the burning bush.

God gives Moses the directives pertinent to the coming assignment. He also gives him a few instructions for immediate execution such as *"Put thine hand into thy bosom."*

Moses obeyed each instruction that God gave. This consistency of obedience is the element that actually opened and grew his capacity for God. As his capacity became greater, God gave more difficult directions to execute.

After Moses learned to acknowledge God, his spiritual GPS (Godly Positioning System) turned on. God downloaded specific coordinates and re-routed Moses back to Egypt.

As I've fore stated, whatever area God leads you to, that place is ultimately designed to give you more insight as to who you are. All of Moses's life, he never acknowledged God.

The inability to acknowledge God positioned him to be inaccurately labeled causing a lack of direction for his life. He was reared in Pharaoh's house from infancy yet lived a false reality.

He had access to anything he desired but was going nowhere. One simple act, however, changed the course of his life. Acknowledgment yielded direction. Tied to the direction or instruction was undisclosed information concerning Moses' true identity.

When he went back to Egypt, Moses released the prophetic word of the Lord. God also used Moses to initiate a prophetic shift in that region via signs and wonders. After following the directions from God, Moses' was able to gather that he was a Prophet according to Deuteronomy 34:10.

If you take into account that the dynamics of his ministry dealt with nations and kings, we can spiritually deduce that Moses was a highly ranked Prophet. Each time he followed God's instruction, his capacity consistently increased ultimately yielding a rank increase.

Moreover, weight, in and of itself, is a powerful entity. Given its position, it has the ability to crush, build, and/or stabilize a thing. I would suggest that you allow the full weight or authority of God, the right to perform His will today.

He may desire to build one thing within you by crushing another. This will ultimately encourage a sense of stability, which is achieved through a strong foundation.

To conclude, prayerfully this reading has stimulated your awareness of the "more of God" He desires to release to you. Although you may be at a good place, in your spiritual walk, there is still a greater depth and height of God you have not seen.

Don't get complacent! Keep pressing towards the mark and striving for perfection because only the **STRONG** will survive!

CHAPTER NOTES:

APPENDIX I

BOOK SOURCES

- Understanding The Dreams You Dream; Milligan, Ira.

- The Prophet's Dictionary; Price, Paula A., Ph.D

MOBILE APPLICATION SOURCES

- YouVersion Bible app

- Dictionary.com app

- Blue Letter Bible app

WEBSITE SOURCES

- Chemistry.about.com; Catholicism.about.com

- http://as1effect.com/blog/what-is-muscle-confusion/

- https://www.monticello.org/site/jefferson/knowledge-power-quotation

- http://www.livestrong.com/article/392136-can-gaining-muscle-make-you-gain-weight/

- https://ultimatesyntheticoil.com/vehicle-oil-and-maintenance/

- http://www.amsoil.com/lookup/auto-and-light-truck/2014/chrysler/town-and-country/3-6l-6-cyl-engine-code-g-erb-e/us-volume/

- http://www.autoeducation.com/autoshop101/oil-change.htm

- https://truckersreport.wordpress.com/2013/09/09/20-insane-but-true-things-about-18-wheelers/

- http://www.amsoil.com/shop/by-equipment/semi-trailer-trucks/

- https://en.m.wikipedia.org/wiki/G-force

- http://www.medicinenet.com/script/main/mobileart.asp?articlekey=80555

- http://www.biblestudy.org/question/why-did-king-david-wait-to-rule-israel.html

- http://theweightofthenation.hbo.com/themes/what-is-obesity

*A*UTHOR'S RESOURCES

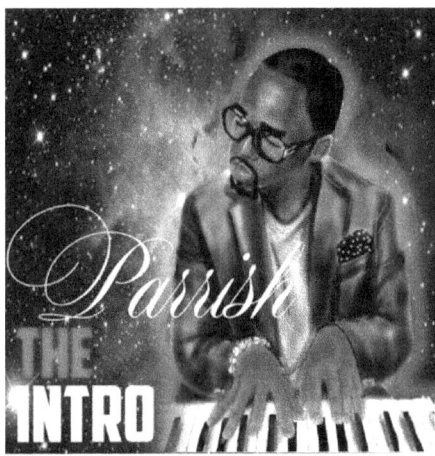

W: www.parrishmiminger.com

Author Contact Information:
E: info@parrishmiminger.com

@MrPMiminger 🅕   @OrganistProducR 🐦